Refuge of the Shallow

poems

brion berkshire

This book is dedicated to the sound
and the silence.

Somewhere

There is a sonnet with your name on it.
Praise is not flattery, a vase not a reliquary
for self adoration. Words are common as the body
adumbrates a shadow. We're vehicles recycling
through light: distance and dissonance. We climb
and recline like morning glory vines. Somewhere,
there is a sonnet. Angel or serpent, your voice
is full of apple blossoms.

-me

This book is a work of fiction. Names, characters, places, and incidents are either products of the author's imagination or are used fictitiously. Any resemblance to actual events or locales or persons, living or dead, is entirely coincidental.

Table of contents

My funny- sad hat

I don't quite know how it came to me-
almost as if it were mine from birth
like being born with a caul hand-
sewn from a minister's shroud
and a too loud Hawaiian shirt;
who knows maybe I swallowed
a rattle full of sorrow and a thimble
full of zeal, or perhaps I had a mobile
in my crib hung with sad clowns
and gay tombstones; or maybe
it was a gift left in my playpen
by a Guardian Jester; its origins
remain unknown as does its purpose
though I once, alone with my lover,
allowed her to look beneath it
at the nothing that sits there
like the holy toad of Buddha,
and all I could say was I will
never make that mistake again.
Now I keep it pulled down over
my ears, my eyes, my sore mouth
so all that shows is the madcap dance
not the levered machine. Some days
I dream of discarding it, of laying
it aside for living a life exposed
to the naked world, but those days
are mercifully short. Most of the time
I'm fascinated by its tiny bronze bells
that both peal and toll, by its earthy
halo of mirth, and how I know it is mine
by its one-size-fits-all occasional charm.

Avian religion

Your parrot sits on his perch and prays
you get run over by a truck. He does this
everyday as soon as your back is turned. He's
tired of saying *Goddamned Republicans*
to impress your liberal girlfriend. And
honestly he hates crackers. Despises them.
At night he dreams and in his dream he roams
in the green parrot jungle making mad parrot
love, line dancing, taking free singing lessons.
The nut he cracks with his enormous beak
against the altar stone
is you, is you.

A satyr in dotage

He used to hang out in lounges
and piss his life away in alleys.
But, man, could he dance with
such abandon he was beautiful
if for no other reason than
his complete, undying belief
that he was. Everyone grew
more free in his presence,
flew about more wildly
in the dark anonymity
of bars, both women
and men frenzied alone
and each other into untold
crazed ecstasies because
they had witnessed his
unrepentant joy. Now,
he lay motionless beneath
the terrible ghosts of sheets,
his still shapely legs and hooves
pinned against the white as if
they were stuck butterfly wings
as he watched the deliciously
formed female attendants fly
about the immaculate room
with that incorrigible rumba
rhythm that always spindled
and thrilled his feral being.
And now it was here, frozen
as he was out of the world
where he had loved so much
and freely, that he understood
the last thing to leave the body
is a small fire, the last kiss
of the insatiable god of want.

Being me

In the story of my life I see myself
being played by the ingénue Angelina
Jolie in drag. I had considered Hilary
Swank because she always wins awards
and who wouldn't want the person
playing them to be a winner

but then again she is so good
at portraying an aching homeliness
and I want my life to be a challenge
so Angelina for me and all the other
characters to be split evenly

between Ed Harris and Meg Tilly
in various stages of attire and disarray,
with maybe a special guest appearance
by Spencer Tracy drunk in a bathtub
of his own waste just because

and then lastly of course I come to you,
the audience, you're so hard to plan for,
sometimes it is difficult to believe
you even exist at all or perhaps
you are really small

no bigger than a postage stamp,
or some mindless floating plankton
just waiting to be swallowed by a whale,
which is fine with me provided

he is played with a practiced nonchalance
by John Malkovich with just a touch
of Woody thrown in for some serious
comic relief

and anyway I think they will be
fine, whoever they are, playing you
as mostly all they have to do is act

as if they are fascinated
by my every passing whim
and, really, how much of
a stretch will that be

as you already
know, being me
yourself.

What's beautiful

You're waiting to be revised
out of the obvious slip-ups,
for someone to erase the debased
portion, the smudge and nudge
of infernal editing, like a grace
to revisit the past, to take these
mistakes and somehow suture
them into a structure both light
and light-giving, something
of an imposed narrative short
sheeted over the awful face
of history, all the while
forgetting

it's the discrepancy
where you fudged the total,
the botched attempt to simulate
the imperfect life, the tiniest
cracks and brushstrokes

that you've fretted over
for hours like the lines
you see growing
imperceptibly
deeper
in the mirror,

that finally make
this art
your own

Catprayer

I used to pray for things to happen
never once realizing how silly it was
as if god were some oddly distant house
cat curled up before a fire, indifferent
to us and our need for her soft rub
but something that we had to coax
to come near us with a small bowl
full of the warm milk of praise,
and that she might, if we petted her
brilliant fur and scratched her fuzzy
head endlessly, she might be pleased
enough to accept our meager adoration
which she neither needed nor desired
but abided because it gave her
a strange feline satisfaction
to know she endured.

the idea of the sensual

of polished wood and desolated space
and the distance the hand must travel
to take in what the eye perceives,
to raise it to the mouth's open cave
or to turn it to the ear's subtle taste,
to allow the essential smell to permeate
or the skin to drink in its grain and finish
in a flourish- every elemental thing contains
this basic most need, the desire a membrane
has to be penetrated, to have its facets known
as love, to be embraced with an ample polish
that throws a shimmer like water over the face--
a veil that manages to salve and save this waste
of a world, again and again, every broken day.

the hourglass figure

They had been going at it hard for quite awhile
when he looked out the window and noticed
the rain falling stealthily through the leaves.
The next time he looked up the leaves were
all gone and it was snowing but then they
were back and it was Spring again. They
had been going at it for an awfully long
time by now and he began to worry a little
about the neighbors, what if they should
call the police, but she said don't worry
the neighbors never call the police here
they just sit looking out their windows
amazed at the fine sand slowly filling
up their veins.

*Braccae illae virides cum subucula rosea et tunica Caledonia –quam elenganter concinnatur!**

Everything sounds more profound in Latin
and ancient, like Satan who, of course,
can only be summoned in such a rich,
sonorous tongue. It calls for hoods
and robes, for blood sacrifices
and other ridiculous rituals.
Not those ungodly pants
and that effeminate shirt
you wear as you stare
down the difficult
left to right, downhill
break against the subtle
grain on that deceptively
perfect and orderly green
of the ninth at the righteously
exclusive and expensive country
club that you joined this summer
to say you belong. You're playing
with Jim, Dave and Father Reed
who secretly keeps a cold one
tucked inside his bag for
'emergency purposes'.
By the eighteenth
he'll be completely
in the bag, like he is
religiously every Saturday
as his preliminary to saying
the evening mass, the mass
you used to love to hear
when you were a child
and knew nothing
of the meaning
but were held
in the spirit
and the body
of the impossibly
articulated syllables
as if this arcane and
glorious language
were God's.

*-roughly translated as *Those green pants go so well with that pink shirt and plaid jacket.*

passing thought

It must be sublime to have come to the end of it,
to have plucked the final word, niggling worm,
from the last leaf of consciousness, to have said it
and know that it is right, not perfectly but finally right,
the importance not in a turn of phrase but in the complete
turning out of the mind, to allow yourself to go mute
as marble, once and for all to be content to be nothing
but content, no longer the vessel but the thing itself,
to be lifted and borne in the solemn air as a voice
freed from the dark tunnel of the throat manifests
itself in sudden waves, to be valued as a possession
minus the self's constant bickering for attention,
but to be attended for the mere presence of form
that recognizes no perishable thing in its demise,
to see yourself de-ranged, set apart and polished
as if the body were the only subject for a change
worth memorializing, with no sense of emptiness
to be kept alive, but mere substance allowed
its properties and propensities toward
a full surrender inside its own gravities;
like the fallen apple, the broken wheel,
or the mutilated carcass of language

ghost in the Polaroid

Flesh is the body's compensation
for the spirit's work. All light to all shadow,
pale worm works through the soft apple,
the burnished nail the grainy wood.

What eats is what remembers
to eat again. The sharp tooth, hunger's
open fist aching for something to grasp.
What moves is what bleeds beneath it.

Here, there is the white fish
on its dark plate. The stone and its fur
of moss. The dropped and the re-clasped.
In the dark air, I hear its clicking. Take.
Re-take.

This is yours.

elegy for the forgotten world

I.

somewhere
there is a heaven
for horses and ducks,
black swans, cormorants
and ruby throated hummingbirds

someplace
I forget just where
there is for notebooks
and pencils, inkblots
and used up words
and especially
erasers

there is one for old
machinery, widgets
and gadgets, winches
in need of retooling,
and that charbroiled
stench off the coils
of motors burnt by
the weird ghost
of electricity

there has to be one for
radiance, dust motes,
flies' overcooked
bodies, rapid rabbit
exhalations

and if there isn't for
a claret of evening sky,
grandmother's knitting
fingers, how warm
the moon is leaning
through a window

something is wrong

how could I forget
compromised promises,
a father's soft lies, blown
ninth inning leads, grace
of the tensionless falling
snapped kite string,

the surprisingly brilliant
pungence of drying
varnish, lost pennies,
misplaced and worn
out identities

and how about
an ant's tragic
logic, a spider's
genius surveying,
the butterfly's
nervous twitch
to be off
earth

and the unused, abused
by neglect, or the impulse
toward bad taste, the body's
coughs and guffaws, back
closets of flannel shirts, air

compressors, factories
producing whoopee
cushions, the urge
towards exuberance,
the buried mountains
of everyday refuse,

sickles of clipped
toenails, the black off
overdone toast, last
Christmas's tawdry
downtown window
treatments,

the also-rans of
spouses, the flushed
spreading rose of Kotex,

skin flecks, cancerous thyroids
and prostates, the destined
fallout of rotting
baby's teeth,

and the darker religions
of stones, the patience
of amoebas, subdural
orbital transversals,
a metal doohickey
off of a Wonder
bread wrapper,
dead

wind, musical notes
after they go beyond
hearing, hairclogs, maps
of varicose veins, where
the mind goes right
before orgasm,

black mollies swallowing
fantail guppies' babies,
squashed ladybugs
that smell bitter
as yesterday's
coffee,

pictures of vague
relatives relinquished
in fire, the ash of
ashtrays, the giddy
vertigo of inhaling
gas fumes,
holy

vomit and excrement.
Jazz and jism. The simple.
The plain. The hard fact
that a rock that sinks
remains on bottom
awaiting

a final accounting

II
in the meantime

perhaps someone should
fashion an old fashioned lean-to,
makeshift a quonset hut for holding
the semi-precious, the near famous,
the far, the small, the indistinct,
the unglamorous that is
swimming all around us

how big would it need to be
to house giant gnat swarms in kudzu,
the spotted alfalfa aphid knee-deep
in shrinking African violets, sperm
whales exalting in plainsight, sea

anemones, polyeurothane containers
slowly decomposing, the what is neither
the first nor last, the caught in betweens
of creation, three and a half legged,
arms foreshortened, balding
carcasses of roadside
couches

or the cast away as useless,
vented spleen and fingerling
appendix, the scrapped plans,
postponed trysts with married
women, or men, or mis-
printed maps for
traveling

into and out of
the unreal world,

or the all too real
sincerity of truly
bad poetry,

blasting

caps, broken Singer
bobbins, baseball cards
of washed up has been
never weres, outmoded
clothes of game show
hosts,

ghosts that haunt old
Philco TVs from the 60s,
the second color sets,
lost opportunities

for a first time, or last
apology, what the sunset
must look like
behind October
clouds

45s, 8
tracks,
nickel
deposit
on 7-

Up bottles,
notions, elixirs
and misplaced
grandeurs, face

cream, bath oil that smelled like
old people, and grandpa's false
teeth in a jar by the 4-
poster

the taste of a railroad
spike after it stopped
raining,

what
it feels like to step
on a thumb tack
or tar

bubbling
up from asphalt
in mid-July heat,

stomach cramps,
aspirins,

the sudden twang
of sardines turn-keyed
out of their metal
caskets,

multi-colored
gravel on the bottom
of fish aquariums,
dinghies, dish
towels, bell
towers,
pterodactyls,

whatever we have
or have not

forgotten, displaced,
walked over, passed
by, left unnoticed as
below contempt or
immaterial or ugly,
some place to store
it all like valuable
antiques and
antiquities

in a shop that never
closes because no
one ever visits
anyway

where
starlight, moonstones,
mood rings, everything
even ordinary dust
is allowed to settle
into place

to wait
for forever
to come along
and give the fallen,
the dispossessed,

the unloved,
the old

heave ho

the migration of angels

who knows exactly when they began
to disappear. Some say it all started
in the beginning and they have been
slowly building towards exodus over
millennia. Others argue that there never
was a beginning. Still others protest
that they were never here to begin
with. It gets confusing. But I know
how real they can be. Like the time
I picked one up hitchhiking. What
a mistake. She was beautiful, make
no mistake about it, and she knew
it too. She said men were always
confusing the effects of beauty
upon their bodies for some sort
of relevant truth. But there wasn't
any, I mean, how could there be?
But god did she go on about herself
and how hard it is to bear the burden
of being HIS emissary, and didn't I
even consider how much need there
was in the world for her kind, how
nothing ever got done without some
assistance like, for instance, the pure
exquisite beauty of her uncanny head
for business, how whole economies rise
and fall with the heavens of her small
breasts, how huge governments collapse
for lack of her intimate knowledge for human
manipulation? She pulled lipstick and compact
out of her voluminous purse and started painting
on her face. Two turquoise doves taking flight
in a whorl of violet sunset. A patina of fading
twilight. She then had the gall to insinuate
that my uncanny skill with the ladies was
somehow 'wind aided'. So I asked her
how far was SHE going. She just motioned
vaguely ahead, into the dark and ominous
future. I rolled up to the curb and let her
out. Took a hard left. She parted indelible
lips and raised her skirt an incredible inch.

how I became so beautiful

it took many millennia
of ancestors' arbitrary

and totally pointless
pursuit of desire

for the ancient debauchery
of each other's bodies

and the bliss of entering
and exiting like breath

as if each moment
held something fragile

as a life which keeps
expanding

and expounding
on the vagaries

of itself which
as we all know

by now is its own
inevitable softness

pushing through
the green singer

who stands
transfixed

between the blue
angel

and the black
light

burning

ugly

is the only word
for the woman you wake up next to
after a long night of heavy Mist
and Coke in a poorly lit
swanless dive.

Or its how
you'll have to face her
and find words to say
prettily

Get your ugly ass out.

But you're not too worried--
you've gotten good at this
sort of thing, practice making
quick work of the imperfect.

It amazes you
how easy it is really
like the time you found
the ugliness that sin is
alleged to be, isn't.

No, that's not what stops
you lathering the mirror's face
or the razor as it burns down
your stubbled cheek,
it's the nagging
sense

it's really you there twisted
in the tangled sheet, your golf-ball
bottom and divoted face that begins
to realize its ungainly shape,

your clumsy body that slips
back inside its wadded bra
and panties, and blinks out

into the harsh light
of another,
ugly day.

the fluke of inspiration

with acknowledgment and thanks to Doug Knowlton for the inspiration

a horror story for ants

Just another sun day on the farm.
Every body was busy carrying bits
of things, a speck of dirt, a dead fly,
a couple were fascinated by a pool
of spit. There wasn't a philosopher
in the bunch, no time to think
or relax, everyone was nervous
and twitchy, watching the sky
for falling shoes just like every
other day. Everyone that is except
Harvey. Harvey had had some pain
in his abdominal area. He had eaten
some mucus balls that he found
under a dandelion runner that smelled,
or what an ant takes for smell, delicious
but now he began to wonder. Maybe there
was something wrong with it, no other ants
ate any, why did they stay away? It would have
been so much easier had the ants developed
a better communication system, but the bulk
of their scientists were still studying that
spot of spit. Suddenly Harve found himself
drawn to a stalk of timothy. *Climb it*
a voice said. *Climb it to the top.*
Attach your mandibles and wait
for a sheep it commanded. He didn't
know what a sheep was and didn't see
a reason to climb but couldn't help himself.
Up he climbed. And waited. The light began
to grow dim. The sun on his face was
as far off and distant as the memories
of his wasted life. Once he had vaguely
sensed a longing for a way, a means
of expressing all the delicate things
that he had felt, all the desires he
had had pass through his sections
but, after all, what could one expect,
he was only an ant. Slowly, a mob

of sheep began to take shape
out of the misty nothingness
that existed beyond the edge
of the known realm and mosey
down the long hill engulfing
all the timothy ahead of it.
Whatever it was
he was waiting for
it wouldn't be long now

wistful thinking

I want to regain my sense of humor
like the old man who takes Viagra
longs to recapture some sense
of the weightlessness of youth,
the strange buoyancy of boyhood
when he could be lifted effortlessly,
and ever so slightly, off
the awful earth, neither
butterfly nor aeroplane
but hovering,
nonetheless

or, like the young woman
who desires her innocence
returned intact, moments after
surrendering to the flamboyant
burning of his, and her, yearning,
yearning for the present
to be rewrapped
or unkindled

but of course, it won't be,
things that are gone
stay gone, there is
no returning

to that time when he floated
out of himself in the delicate coracle
of her presence, his lithe limbs oaring
toward some shore, the permanent
anchors of time and gravity
momentarily unchained,

and innocence, that dumb
avian, once he's flown
there's no sense coaxing
him back with soft coos
or coy promises of cool
water and stale saltines-

what's lost tends to remain
so- and, as everyone must
admit, there is nothing

funny in that

unless, of course,
it is laughing
at our indomitable
propensity

toward
wistfulness.

short stories for the long night

We had no light colored
parasol and it was
raining a ton
of darkness.

A flea and a cockroach
slip into the bar as
a priest and a rabbi
stumble out. In eerie
neon their shadows
touch like shy lovers.

In the corner sits a madman
scribbling War and Peace
onto a matchbook cover.
Later, he'll mistranslate it
into French on a fraction
of crushed eggshell.

A trapezoid of moonlight
was trapped on the bedroom
ceiling. There would be no escape.
In the morning it would be dead
like so many other things.

The day flows gray and unlovely
as the wizened woman's hair
the beautiful mortician's
daughter combs out slowly
humming softly to herself.

The cat in the corner
smiles at the gray
mouse it is about
to eat.

Midwinter and Heraclitus's
river has frozen over.
An old man and his
lonely son skate
its blurry surfaces
to the widow's cottage
that's boarded up
until Spring.

You feel yourself falling
apart over coffee. I am going
to pieces, you say,
to your ashes
in the ashtray.

A stranger comes in
looking for a sign.
What's he doing here?
He stands perplexed
between the men's
room and exit.

A certain Mr. Black
waits and fidgets
with his weskit.
Doesn't he know
no one dresses
like that anymore!
He refuses to believe
she isn't coming back,
his coy mistress,
the 19th century.

the koan of Michael standing

for Michael Corr

It’s clear the grain
will outlast him.

Inside the blue lave
of rain, she loosens

her obi to know
the warm in wet.

He watches her
sighs, and heaves,

leaning hard on
a scythe. He'll have

to work to stretch
what is left to bind

inside a tapering
sleeve of minutes.

She moves through
amber swatches

of sintering autumn
as drying sheaves

go slowly sepia.
They’ll merge

somewhere in half
light sidling

as day slips
like an ellipsis

inside its dark
sentence,

a chiaroscuro
purer than memory.

morning wood

Perhaps it takes place under water:
The delicate displacement of want
brought forth into the light of day:
What was it I could have been

dreaming: a young woman bicycling
downhill, her bare feet spinning in ever
quickening circles, more and more
out of control until she was nothing

but shivering speed as lucid as dark;
or that other fully rounded and jumping
rope shirtless, or the twin girls twirling
the braided cord in graceful loops

as she bounds unbounded between them?
And where am I in this subdural French
projection pregnant with cliche'd symbolism,
writer, director, and audience all in one

masculine, maculate trinity? I startle
awake, unaware of what has been taking
shape below, sub-marine, only conscious
of an uncomfortable stiffness, tucked in

a sling of cotton as if it were a broken limb
anxious to be healed, or at least brought
into the presence of some body of light
and water, some magnetic point pulling

my own being's inner compass, relentlessly
in pursuit of a destination I would know at once
as true north, a place among the worlds to wake
up new, and fresh as the original, primeval forest.

Watching the ifc

We're sitting in this movie theatre
holding hands in the dark
only there isn't any
dark, it's light
and there's no movie
theatre only more
of the same

and we aren't sitting
we're running
along the banks of some
crazy river and there's careening
trees and zany birds only

we aren't running
we're merely walking
and the crazy river is
just some dirty clothes

I left lying
and the trees careening
and those birds
are all outside
the opaque window
the wind
rushes past

but there isn't any past
there's just this now
we have to deal with
and it's rushing too
fast too

oh yeah and we aren't
walking and there really aren't
any dirty clothes
I just made that up
I'm really a good house
keeper from the
1950's, all blown up
bouffant and pregnant

but of course
there isn't any real
baby, it's make believe
it's TV, I love Lucy
but I don't really

care for the neighbors
and anyway it's later
than it seems so
later I'll take a bath
or undo my hair

but there really isn't
any need so why bother
I don't none of this is real
except for the scary parts
there doesn't seem
to be any plot

to any of this
just the eye of
the camera recording
what rolls by, only
there isn't any
film

and no direction
and where did you go
I thought we were holding
patterns only there isn't any
on/off there's just volume

to be filled up
only there is no up
there's only there
and anyway

we aren't going up
there this time we're going
to stay put and see what
comes but there isn't

anything coming there's
something but it won't budge
and anyway it's too late

for us, too late for anything
and besides

there isn't any need
to worry you are alright
and it doesn't matter
if you aren't

cause you're really
not real or here
I'm alone

Prayer of me

Lord, make me
an instrument:

A blue flute,
a green lyre,
a red tambourine.

Make me a hollow
womb that gives birth
to echoes.

Lord, make me over with
valves and levers. Give me
a bell-shaped horn

or make me electronic!
A thing that changes tone
under the lightest touch,

or that can be tuned into
an ensemble at the flip
of a switch. Lord,

I wish to be re-fabricated
a tangible instrument,
capable of being

mastered by a delicate
hand, to have both
melody and harmony

brought forth from me
effortlessly. Work me
with a flawless

precision, craft me
under a well-known
name so I will remain

desirable. Allow me
an increase in value
over time like a

Stradivarius or a Gibson
Les Paul. Give me lasting
shape that invites

both the caress
and strum. Oh Lord, bliss
and bend me

into a musical-
giving instrument
in this dark world

where song is
always the means
and end

of salvation.

The dog of his body

wants more sleep than he gives,
more food than allowed, more sex

than is quite necessary, *thank you*
very much. It longs to curl up on hearths,

to chase the rare rabbits, to snooze in the warmth
of a familiar lap. It knows what it knows by following smells,

by taste, by sudden touch and sound. It wears an odd half-circle
in the yellow grass at the end of its hardened chain. Summers, it sheds

its fine hair, lolls its thick tongue, naps in the dark shade of the pine trees.
Some days it sits on the top of the house contentedly; other nights, keeps

the neighbors awake with a lonesome baying. Though there seems something
sad stuck deep in its marble eye, it is amenable to a tender training by swift yank

on the leash, the smack on the nose of the great newspaper, or a loved voice
in the night crying Heel! Heel! *O Heal, O great beast of memory, bearer*

of the long history of hunger and need, run free in the open
space for awhile, chase the ghosts that haunt your dreams

beneath fences, across wide fields and dim-lit orchards,
follow what light there is inside your happy barking

heart, run away from this shadowy thing that waits
for your unlikely return beside your overturned dish,

your silver, oversized bowl.

A man who writes poems

is playing in the dark
5,10,15,20
it is late
and he is tired
25,30
he has lain spooning alongside
the periphery of things. he has
touched the rough sewn backs
of chairs, the corseted lining
black inside closets
35,40,45
he has lounged with spiders
behind the Barcalounger
couched in silence. stilled,
his rivening breathing
still betrays
55,60,65
he has been found pretending
he might blend with rich patterns
of oak panels, with the sheer opacity
of curtains, beneath the masks
and costumes, dying
70,75
to ape a curve
of shadow
80,85
he has slid into the obvious
spaces between, or under
he has hid behind
his own hands
90
now he stands before
a mirror,
opens and closes
95
his eyes, dissolve
and release
100
the stuttered image
turns and returns
ready or not

and he is gone again
here I come
to seek the place
where the other is

Zenith to nexus to nadir

1

Awaiting abandonment, I sit and listen-
hear nothing.
Life comes in ebbs and flows,
and then passes quietly,
leaving behind the crumpled pasta shells
which we have come to believe in
as our prescient bodies, nest of the hummingbird
and the stumbling bee
buzzing the hive of the mind with an endless quest
for the sweet and sour of summer flower nectar;
an open emptiness, oblivion of satiation.

2

Outside my varicose window absence
takes up space intended for other things,
frozen flower stems and sentient shafts of summer grass
deconstruct under the cold, watchful winter sun,
making room for a lot of nothing, in particular:
Indeed 'nature adores the vacuumed room'
to move her stunningly new green
spring and summer fashions into-
a blank slate, a clean space to re-create in.

3

There is a subtle music in silence sometimes,
glassy ocean song of the mind gone caesura,
the emptying air is heir to every known resonance
such as we have learned to discern from
the bodies of plucked guitars and strummed women,
the hollowness reverberates with something

4

also found in conch shells and pop bottles
drawn over by the wind's invisible bow,
or by the sudden cessation of her hands

on the shaken boughs of the ash tree-
A voice says curl into yourself and be still-
as the last frost-chilled leaf stubbornly clings
to its precarious perch, in search of time's delayed blessing
to permit a fall gracefully in

5

Later, as night lays her lacquer over everything,
beneath a sky sequined with stars,
we explore and exploit caverns of dream,
stalactites and stalagmites of symbols hang there useless
as a hollowed hall of fantastically impotent phalluses,
'til we loosely render each lucid
by naked implication and fragmented disassociation.

6

Here, there is the constant wish for history.

The testicle in his tender shell, husky, musky fruit,
consistently sits and plans the inevitable dissolution,
inveigling eyes to see and hands to finger-touch
a distance, a hair's breadth where there is room still
to breathe, a philosophy of the long ago burning bed
of slow flowing rivers; the left behind of streams, stones, memories of water.

7

Another brilliant day, guilty by proxy.
Inside the unbroken light, I fan out and sun.
Sipping too sweet tea at the cobwebby, forenoon window,
a line on the near grass patched with tan is a secret signpost,
and a fulcrum against an unbalanced unknown.

8

I move through the day and night equally replacing displaced air,
denying and reaffirming dizzying presence endlessly through
emptiness, I fall and rise, rise then fall
from zenith to nexus to nadir, a wave passing
over and am always replaced, more and less
and again, more or less

9

Outside, inside the sunlight, birds.

10

Truly, the mystical world of casual birds that loaf
and the intricate arachnid patterns which exist
pressed between panes of undusted glass are inexplicable,
archaic as grandmother's end-table's handmade lace,
and as beautiful as a slow intake of breath,
or sorrow.

11

I still wish for a small secret garden somewhere
where I can stroll a monk among silent stones and statues,
where I may lie down on damp earth, feel the cool richness enter my body
and smell my smell in its smell, my touch in this tethered embrace;
a garden which might also come to imply a clearing
away of the unnecessary. I pick up a straw

12

broom and whisk dead bees
like last summer's leftover thoughts
from the corners on my screened-in front porch,
and am satiated by emptiness.
As if an ancient, archaic god,
who is indeed no-thing, replicates no images
without pause, in pauses, fills in with emptiness
another silent afternoon where I am now

13

awaiting abandonment,
carefully I sit and listen
and hear nothing

I can add anything to

Echo

Resounding echo

But what if you did get me
pregnant, wouldn't that be amazing and a little bit scary
like being famous, and we would be, knowing tabloids
and their lust for the stunning
headline

and what would it be like to look down
and know I was carrying someone alive
in me like a secret becoming less
well kept over time,

a secret someone touching
parts of me I'd never see

and just think of the people
stopping by and saying things like
Congrats! and *Jehosophat!*
Do you have a name yet?
And us saying well
we thought of Summer
and Autumn

Skye but now we're leaning
toward Aphasia
Annabelle or Echo
Lalia because

we want her simple and smart
and sound.

And the people walking away
frowning

How we would love that and the appointments
with the nurses saying this will be cold
and it is, and the doctor not seeing
exactly what to exam

But what if there's something wrong

what if he says hmmm, or that's unusual
or we'll have to do more tests
and what if she has only one kidney
or a split in her spleen or no heart
beat. Now that would be rare
and sad, but she would be still
beautiful in a blue repose
like you.

She'll be fine
probably, medical science
advances rapidly and there's the law
of averages which she'd rise above
having numbered toes and fingers
and that same muffled thump
that aches in all of us
and keeps us up nights

And of course there's the ultrasound
telling them useful facts
like does she have a penis-
Well there are worse things
she could have

but anyway, the time would come
and you would be worrying about
in tweeds, while I fawn in floral
as if I were a giant cascade aching
to break, and cursing you,

the doctor, god, and three other people
I don't know, until she finally finds her
way out, thank stars, and takes her first
mouthful of air and gives it back, an aria
of open vowels, full of her own force
of life, and then we'd find
she'd already begun

translating her world
into sound

Return of echo

songs on the baby monitor

I call you infant after
the Latin *infans*

meaning unspeaking
because you are

unspeaking as a phone
sans earpiece, or a mute
template

for yearning. I machine
an elegance for your ultimate
ululation.

You're pure oeuvre,
blue baby, garnerer
of vulgar sonorities.

I lend you this,
my final strain
and cadence.

A haven for vacua
and moral valences,
you're great.

I listen for you
to aspirate

Heart of echo

Sometimes it takes delicate instruments
to detect something so faint as a *mur mur*,
a slight variation in the normal rhythm

that indicates there's something wrong
somewhere, maybe a hole in a wall
or a leaking valve, and sometimes

you can live with it for years with no
effects, like a man having a guardian
angel or a secret admirer

and it might take something dangerous
as a heart attack before you know something
is there, and then occasionally it will be

too late and then you just wring your hands
and say so sad so sad, but sometimes
the delicate instruments report something

that really isn't serious or life threatening
something we really don't know why
it's there or what causes it, just another

mystery and then we're left wondering
how this strange echo has affected us
so are we different for having this odd

throb that no one can hear not even
us but the instruments keep stammering
away it's, it's there, or is this just a minor

oversight in our making, a leftover flutter
from some ancient wing someone forgot

Wish for echo

May you only grow
so lonely as to fall in love
with yourself; spelunk shadows
of secret places for the source
of self deceit, learn to span
the breadth of reach
and grasp, and
the how to of
letting go.

May you be uncommon
as strawberries or asparagus
or juniper berries, and live in
constant awe of icicles,
chrysanthemums,
surrendering.

May you glean oddball nature
for a perfect breathing; uncover
your undisclosed genius
for orgasms

in the presence
of ordinary things.

Water

Life under water

I.

He remembers his first wet dream
taking shape under the delicate cover
of water: swimming through impossible
weightless shifts of blue

armless as an eel, and dazzling
between her hairless legs legions
of white incredible, all the while
her weirdly transfixed face

smilingly molting from Lara
to Esmerelda, light sifting
from a cold cobalt basalt
to sapphire.

II.

Sound carries better there
where meaning disappears.

He was progressing slowly,
sometimes vapidly, against

the subtle irresistible
charm of undertow.

He discovered breathing
came easier the longer

he managed to remain
submerged.

III.

He was dying again
as he knew he should be.

He came up and gulped
large mouthfuls of air,

a momentary reprieve
from languid liquidity,

then dropped back
a whale.

IV.

Zen-like, he sits
on the soft bottom,
thinking through the giving
muck. At forty-five, he recalls
the ignorant innocence of fourteen,
the denouement of a secret
water that still stains
and holds him
under.

Negative water

It is important to remember
it is the leaf takes the light
and does something valuable
with it. Not the poet's hand

which piles verbiage upon
foliage to forest a lusher
landscape. Nor may words
catabolize the dead like water.

We cannot denature nature
nor ourselves. Still, we can
erect epigrams, lick nipples
to profundity, massage a cleft

or tower to some higher
purported purpose; in a word
we manipulate. Make use of
others' incorrigible otherness

we find outside which fixes
us to our own ubiquitous
uniqueness. It is important
to remember

we are not less than
what we are, either.

Drifting through water

My father saw turtles when there
weren't any there. He said look, see
those turtles there. I lied I said yes
I see them there. He said they've been
behind us, those turtles, for quite some
time. I said yes dad I see. He said those
turtles are following us, disappearing
and re-emerging from behind each wave.
I said yes dad. He said watch those turtles
stay just beyond reach. I said yes. Now
rest dad. Slowly, a dark head sunk
behind the boat I was struggling
just to keep afloat.

Skin diving

Begin at the head

cut through the tough
crusted scalp, part the hairs

permanently. Then lob off
the soft lobes of ears,

and further, sculpt off
the face, being careful not

to upset the set of the eyes,
down the down-turned nose

to the querulous mouth
with its quivering lips

about to shout Stop!,
and even further

the hose of the neck,
rack of shoulders,

the down covered cage
of the heart, the empty plate

of the belly, the shivering hair
of the groin, carefully remove

the testes from its wrinkled shell,
spoon out the hips

like a morning grapefruit,
the delicately pouting anus,

strip the cylindrical thighs
of their smooth clothes,

slide over the hard knobs of the knee,
the tangle of tendons like a scaffolding,

down the half-moons of the calves,
hubcaps of the ankles,

the frail starfish of metatarsals,
to the sad, papery face of the sole,

and still the self-knife hungers
for more shimmering skin

to be torn away, more removals
to find what depths lie beneath

for me to dive further into.

Taking on water

I have been lying low
for awhile. Under the inverse
of images, faces ignore me in self
contemplation. It's a cliché to say

I am sleeping: rather I am thinking
so deliberately as to appear
immutable. Like a blind god
my one eye never blinks.

What has time to do with anything?
Eternity's beyond me. I am turning
things over, mulling my options
below the knowable surface.

Cold and hot are related, slowly,
by degrees. My indifference
to everything is pure, my one,
lasting satisfaction. I live, if

it can be said, real and concrete
as any world, as the relentless
fluidity which forever slips over
persists in its pallid exertion

to wash me more smooth.

Becoming vessel

The tree begins this voyage in violence. To be chosen
is to be broken, to know the awful grace of awl
and axe, the elegant stroke of the saw's tooth
effortlessly eating away the pith.

What's left is hollowed, a space for air
to allow a certain buoyancy, a tendency
toward floating over after the removals
and final, articulated shavings;

to be reformed by the unseen into a hull
for the carrying of an unknown cargo,
loaded ceaselessly by the merciless
hands of the un-shriven world,

and to even know a light sense
of gratitude for the weight that's
granted; and then, with a boon
such as luck, to be borne over
water by a gift of wind.

He casts his nets in brilliance

or near darkness, there is the momentary
spinning whoosh and then the soft
thud of entering another

world made of water; an instantaneous
added gracefulness as if it were a living
thing, a being slowly filtering down,
an angel, perhaps, minus wings
or signs of the obvious
trappings of faith.

Hauling up is another matter.

The steady pull and constant strain
on forearms, feet splayed wide
in a false belief of attaining
some credible sense
of balance,

and the rough, wet rope
bringing to his hands the true
callousness of the known world,
as it gracelessly, reluctantly
slowly hands over

the ancient lives of fishes
into the unaccountability of sunlight
and death-- their startled eyes staring
and their thick mouths drowning
on air--

and then the flying vee as he heads back
into the dark he came from, the perfect split
of seam where two universes ultimately touch
and bleed into one

Angling for ease

It was something I had to learn,
the practiced patience of waiting
for the line to complete its full sweep
and the frozen s of the leader

to begin to unfurl; learn to breathe
a second posed with tip high, body
and rod one, flayed backwards,
tense yet relaxed as a sprinter

set in his blocks; and then the smooth
transition, everything flowing forward,
up and over, the hand a pivot across
the arc of the circle, the weight shift

perfectly timed, the snap of the wrist
and the final follow through; the fly
retracing its airy path gracefully,
the swish and then the soft thud

on the water; learn the egoless
confidence of a divine execution,
and never forget the unmuttered
prayer

there be no backlash.

No future in the past

Broken open in history

It was the hinge of a door
when you left me. A door
closing down like a small fire
that has come to know destiny
in its own intricate unraveling,
a fire which is cold and burns
like the infamous past
and what are we made of
but curiously glowing embers
frozen out and locked in place?
Still, there's that perfect hinge
that says here, here is where
your life swung unhinged
magically, a screen door afloat
on a gyring river, the same one
that escapes twisting through
the sacked and abandoned
landscape, scarred and sacred
as a burned out trailer park
where a fat lady with a cane
and glass eye knows exactly
the price and cost of every
known and necessary thing,
-*and wouldn't I care for some*
sweet tea? -as she pirouettes
gracefully for one painfully
useless eternity and opens
just a bit as if I had been
expected all along
to pass through

Margaret

It is New Year's Day,
1852, the same year
I am going to die.
I don't know that yet.
My future husband fidgets
under his freshly starched
collar. He will leave me here
in the ground come September,
head out west to California
with his two brothers

chasing the gold
of sunsets. Who knows,
maybe he finds some.
The brothers will die
en route, one of Typhus,
the other robbed, beaten,
and stabbed. I won't know
any of this. I'll only know
how lovely I look in mother's
chiffon and lace, my barely
more than a girl saucer
blue eyes veiled

to what awaits
on my wedding night
and further on. I am light
as the sifting snow swirls
through the churchyard
graveyard. The same
I will lie in later
this autumn,

in this same snow
white gown, dreaming
my perfect children playing
in the late afternoon half-
light before my dream
house, Nathaniel slanting
slowly across the sun
burnt field, his golden
arms laden with plenty.

Jesus and Venus

he wooed her through his nightmares,
through the long desert days he lay enticed
to give himself over, and what should be
the harm in that?, taking a luxuriant bath

in lucid, wavering flesh, the joy and grace
of instant pleasure, the way one would choose
to lose the thick mind's incumbent weight
and pray alone through nerves and pores

for glory where there is no need for double
crossing the bawdy body hungers, where he
is no longer bereft of need but, finally, comes
at ease in long fluent strides towards release-

there is quiet in the smudged sand and the moon
reveals and revels in the lizard's shuddered awakening
and the open bank of stars stops promising
anything other than pure vistas that stretch

the ubiquitous universe beyond belief
into whatever shapes one imagines, coiled
or spiraling off in shivering rivers of heat, which,
as they cool, congeal themselves into shadow

A small animal like grief

works all morning just outside of eye shot,
incessant in its quest for a place for wintering over,

scurries about for a warm spot to burrow in and bury
its inscrutable face, sniffs through the rotting leaves,

the dying grass for a place to shudder in an opening,
shoulders through and circles about the floor

as if it were making itself a home, as if it were
planning on a long stay. And I, as pliant as earth,

accept as anything of this tiny warmth,
its softness hollowing inside of me a nest

for the birthing of shadows, long tunnels
to house its mammalian echo.

Character, actor

He continues improvising
having lost the sacred script
but an impersonated life
is all about back-story
and he held to his routinely.
He knew, for instance, that love
remained a brutal angel of mercy
somehow beyond grasp. Perhaps
it was a secret missing something
someone forgot to whisper to him
or some other thing he mistakenly
forgot. He kept copious notes
about family, friendship, hope,
betrayal. In the fragile margins
he scribbled dubious integrity,
uneven morals and dream-
spook. It was written
somewhere that he broke
once when he was young,
a vague and unfocused
sort of break that no one
ever spoke of. It was as if his life
were formed of finite glass, so thin
that the light that poured through
could shatter him with a mere shake
like a gentle wind on waking skin, so
he avoided the possibility of satiety
as if it were the sad, sodden plague
that it is. He kept thumbing through
the blank pages of an unnamed book
looking for some word that would,
finally, say, that it was now time
and he hadn't entirely missed
his last cue to go on, though
aware that an awkward
silence would still be
somehow completely
and honestly
in character.

Bob Hicok makes another die

in Ann Arbor on a Tuesday, noon,
spinning like the rest of us on the lathe
of God. He hones a vision on a diamond
point, the shearing away a form of formal
separation of the finally useful from what
was merely possible. He watches the maker
adjust his delicate calibrations. The filings
keep spiraling off in long graceful tracings,
the beautiful useless piling up at his feet
like garlands or garnishes. The die man
takes no notice, fixes instead on undying
circumambulations of time and overtime,
watches clocks and waits for a signal
it'll be over soon. Bob looks in on
the finished product, jots notes
for improvements, modifications
for a future reference, draws
his own conclusion. What he
makes of what it is he is
handed is life,
is art, is all.

A moose in the heart

stands knee deep in marshgrass,
water rainbowing off his beard,
and browses the bottomlands
for barks and twigs, slowly
reconsidering. Sometimes he
swims for miles, though clumsily,
and only out of necessity,
to reach the sweeter,
greener leaves. He stomps
the solid ground and groans
from down within the hairy bell
of his arching throat, his terrible
aloneness echoing across
the brilliant lake and out
into wilderness

A true heartpiece

you say I used to say beautiful things to you
and I say I used to write beautiful poems, too.

But I don't now. Why is that? It's as if all this
were being scribbled by some priest who long ago

gave up the trappings of faith but still holds
on to the rituals as his only known source

of eternal income. And perhaps I am a madman
pretending to be perfectly sane and genteel

or not, or I am just so tired and worn out by
this life of epic disappointments that no

vestment fits me anymore. Maybe, maybe
my sweet parishioners have long since

abandoned this church and I am preaching
my homily of old snow and house sparrows

to the stained glass of an empty shell.
Maybe I have become mean and small

as an ugly child who wants with his hands
but cannot reach the lovely joys that drop

so easily to the others. Late at night, when
the recently defrocked priest lays his body

into the grave of his bed, and all the weight
of this life just floats out of him, what is he

left, there in the shadowy world of his restless
existence, where nothing is, and the silences

are so high pitched and terrible that they cannot
be heard, and the moon falls through the window

heavy as a headstone.

Man pleads guilty in death of lovely

I must confess I could never
bring myself to read about it.
I was too lost in considering
just what his delicate motives
might be. She must have come
to hurt him somehow, perhaps
he arrived home too early one
dark evening and found her
drenched in another's frothy
moon-spray, with only a play
of blissful spittle still
clinging to her over kissed
lip. Or maybe she was that
calloused, used up by more
than the unlovely hands of
the many who would have
stripped and scarred her
and so unwittingly
laughed at his withering
brittleness. Or perhaps
he had stumbled in blindly
to find her lying back in
a glistening pool of black,
absently fondled the tactile
knife blade as they do sometimes
in B movies, lost in the shock
of his sudden aloneness.
Perhaps he was taken in half
consciously, admitted guilt
through the gauze of his grief
and gave himself over, with
little or nothing or no one
left to redeem him. Perhaps.
But I have come to suspect
they took the wrong man
in custody.

Muse in state

When death arrives brilliantly, little
by late, the body patiently gives up
its portion of dark. The fragile shell
shimmers emptily, relaxed as any man
after orgasm, hollow and washed clean
in the salt of magnificent oceans. How
radiant the finality of the captured flash
of flesh frozen in place, the face
without question a picture

as lovely as an unresolved potency
left for someone else's need to delve
deeper inside the glamour of despair.
It is here where one, stripped
of the awful husks of dream,
glows as if skin itself were
made of cold light, like
the dead moon, all calf-
white and fogged out,
and full of a quiet

more perfect
than elegy.

Boo forever

Mother in the dark making vague
charcoal sketches of her own shadow.
Father snoring lightly on the couch.
They are waiting there still
for something important
to happen. So quiet,
even the famous violins
of the crickets are shamed
into a vast silence.

You and I on the doorstep
about to ring the doorbell
in our homemade masks
of impenetrable sorrow
and absolute need.

Trick or treat.

Beneath the 'scape of sound

You are beautiful
for a moment the way
some faces are beautiful
in mid-morning light
but later turn ugly
towards early afternoon
it's the same as symmetry
is and the rule of thirds
to some or how a black
squirrel ribboning across
a gray highway becomes
more than a lucid memory
you can't quite let go
of, and you stop for awhile
to reflect upon nothing
really which stretches out
its impossibly long arms to
hold you, and you understand,
finally, what it means to have
earned the uneven pitfalls
of your naked face, somewhere
between the aural magnificence
of language and the moral
ambivalence of silence.

Burning the self an effigy

Take the blue-topped head
of the match in your fingers.
Admire its perfect architecture.
Now hold the cardboard box
firmly in your other hand,
away from your cold self.
Turn it so the *This Side Up*
and *Keep Away from Children*
faces you. Prepare yourself.
Now you're ready. Move
the swollen, the beautifully
sulfur impregnated end to
the rough, rouged surface.
Angling the shank, slowly
drag the nib across the long
tableaux of the checkered
facade. Watch as it flashes
flame, the blue then sudden
orange, red, yellow shift
through expressions. Now
lower it until it is upside
down, and twirl so the fire
spirals up the long shaft,
the ball rising away from
the red and black bloom
of the cooling, bulbous tip.
Let the voracious animal
of heat feed on the little
wooden matchstick-boy
of the body until it scorches
your bony fingers, and even
longer until you smell your
own flesh begin to cook,
then shake it out and drop it
into the open mouth of the sink
where it will hiss and perish
in the dirty-gray water
of the breakfast dishes.
After, turn and walk out
into the morning light as
if something had changed,

as if you had shed something
like skin, as if that smell scouring
your nostrils were the scent of regret
or guilt leaving, and you were free
to take your place, again
in the ash-strewn world.

No see ums

Suddenly, they're everywhere and as
they are so named you can't see them
but they make their presence known
by nibbling you as if you were some
rare and exotic cheese. Like hungry
ghosts they cannot get enough
of the precious camembert of
your unprotected flesh, or perhaps
they are more likely the shape
and form that unrequited regret
takes on, the teeth of your past
floating unseen until they bite you
squarely in the ass. At this point
it doesn't matter what they are
or how they got in through
the impossibly small holes
in the screens that you check
every year for possible breaches.
Who knows maybe they don't even
come in from outside, maybe they
materialize immaterially out of
the nothingness around you, some-
how your life or lack thereof has
provided them with the necessary
impetus to become. Whatever, they're
here and making themselves felt only
too well. You get up and spray about
in the absolute fullness of a faith
that the invisible, too, can be killed.

The secret life of clothes

They carry the memory of your scent
in the folds and creases, the sear
of salt and the dark stain. After
a languorous swirl in the tidal spin,
they tumble through hot afternoons,
then open to the cooling presence
of your legs and arms again. They
ride roughshod over your ruly hair
and down the brambled slope
of your rolling chest. You tug them
up thick thighs which they snuggle
lovingly and over the uneven rounds
of your flared buttocks. They cover
the secret parts of you, those that
make you uncomfortable, the bulges
or concavities, and the dazzling beauty
of clustered flesh. Though you seldom
notice, they lay splayed all day against
your bare body with the intimacy
reserved for a lover or mother.
You do sometimes glance at them
in mirrors or windowed reflections
but only to see how well they hide
your naked imperfections. Their joy
lies in those sudden flashes when
you smile un-self-consciously
damn, do I look good

Soul in space

Jackson says the quicksilver corner,
who correctly reads the wary minnows
of the qb's eyes and picks his safe
dump off in the flat and takes it back
to the house untouched slicker than
a handful of oily water escaping
a three-year old's laughing grasp,
has good hips, good as if their
relative value were virtually virtuous.
Perhaps they are like the blessed hips
of the mother of our savior, spreading
the O of eternity's mouth to the absolute
limit, beyond the point of credulity,
making an opening large enough for
the safe passage of god's ungodly
round head, his massive shoulders,
and the quick pop of the rest of him,
the small bulge of his stomach, his
uncircumcised penis, his sad, papery
testicles, his own lithe hips, those
spindly legs and perfect specimens
of his miniature feet and hands
which years later will be turned
into the velvety blooms of roses
of ultimate forgiveness. Griese
points out the sprinting split end
who has cleared out the zone
behind the backpedaling backers
and then curled in front of the
dropping safety, was uncovered
and, had the harried qb found him,
is very dangerous in open space.
Anyway, the whole play ran in slo-mo
reveals the tackle's hold on the lumbering
tight end which negated the apparent td
the jauntily gyrating corner is still celebrating,
the ubiquitous yellow flag lying on the ground
as if it had been dropped there by a passing
maiden of yesteryear, in the naive hope
her intended might notice it, and her,

and stop, and pick them both up,
and thus begin the unending living
cycle of plays, the intricate,
formal formations,
the interminable planning
and re-planning, the half-
time adjustments to be
mulled and blandly
analyzed over
and over, etcetera
by our inveterate crew
until the final gun sounds
and we can all go to bed
and lie hip to hip, again
filling in the other's
open spaces.

The last erection

Who knows when it will come
or what will be its mysterious
source. Will the cock be aware
this is the last stand, the final
un-wrinkling before the ultimate
unraveling? And will the balls
understand that this is it for
them too, their usefulness
gone in a flash leaving them
to hang there like last
year's overripe apples?
Not to mention the heart
which has a need for this
as a depository for excess,
or the lonely mind which
takes refuge here from
the intimate inadequacy
of language? And what will
the body have to say about
this inherent self knowledge,
the ability to reproduce itself
frittered away like the story
of the beautiful girl who had
so many suitors she could not
make up her mind and died
an embittered spinster?
Or maybe the significance
of this will be grandiose,
maybe there will be bells
and whistles, maybe it's what
the body has been building
towards the whole of life,
the expression of an inner-
most world made clear and
towering if only for a moment-
after which comes the inevitable
collapse like the spent casing
of a shell cast off noisily
unto the hardwood floor,
the alchemy of its dying
bullet having penetrated
and struck deeply inside
its sole, intended mark.

I want to be borne again

on an updraft of wind like the rain is
inside a dark womb of cloud. I want to
be carried inside a pocket and fingered
like a key-ring or quarter occasionally,
nervously as if my being there brought
some odd sort of comfort. I want no
more the anchor of gravity, gravitas
of living, and having lived, the bitter
cigarette of regret burning the tongue.
I would also request the slightest twinge
of sweetness once in awhile, something
sharp and singular like lightning, striking
the shins against the forgotten ghost
of the coffee table in the dark. Maybe
a few words like a talisman to ward
off loneliness, or to invoke a truly
coherent light, a more sustainable
lucidity. While we're at it, I could
use several brand new orgasms
of incorporeal experience, rare
and incomparable where I
might then exhaust the rest
of my inexplicable existence.
Afterwards, when emptiness
equates to brilliant nonchalance,
I wish to be nothing but the rain
again coming down in torrents
and running off in rivulets that
merge into creeks and streams
that river and carve their strange
lineage across the homely face
of the earth, once more a slave
to my own maternal nature.

In this time near the end of days

A man sometimes would fall in love
with his tools. The sure heft in the hand
of the crescent wrench, the multi-utility
of the adjustable spanner, the star-like
quality of the hex key, the perfectly locked
jaw of the well-named Vise-Grips. Slowly,
he would begin to see his marriage, his life,
his family as one enormous breathing machine
in need of constant maintaining. Some days
would only require a good greasing
of the gears, while others demand
the use of more specialized devices.
The Wife Crescent, The Adjustable
Family Spanner, The Vise-Grip
on life. Some nights he would lay
awake and listen in the near dark
for an odd sound, some flaw
in the purring, a muffled tick,
an unexplained wheeze lost
in the works and wonder
what new marvelous instrument
of mechanical precision
he would now have to invent

Waiting for word

I've had a falling out
with the metaphysical.

Temporal as a blown
glass exhibit or an exit
visa, I plot ultimate routes
of escape down the same
avenues of complaints

and the faux pearls
of seasons I've always
mistakenly taken.

It's come to this, then.

A dog barks. Someone pecks piano
keys. Last-light is a distant ship
night submarines.

Cassiopeia, the Pleiades, Orion swash
buckles in for another evening's quiet
display of dispassionate beauty.

Transcendence is rarer than a Rottweiler
falling asleep beneath the glittering
arms of Andromeda. I disappear inside

the post office. My box is empty.
There's no letter explaining
everything. No word
from someone threatening
conciliation.

No bills and no blank
checks. No new shut-
off notices.

Nothing tonight
is overdue.

After omega

No one knew what to do
as this was the final future
everyone had talked about
and fretted over for so long.
People milled around in
small groups, whispering.
A small girl began to sing
to herself about a baby
falling out of a tree.
Her mother said *Stop*
that nonsense, Louise.
Everyone agreed it had
been a beautiful sunset.
The most beautiful ever
most nodded agreeably.
Someone then mentioned
television, how they really
had loved the surreality
of Reality TV. And all
those lovely talk shows
someone else sighed.
And the ballgames,
several men exclaimed
simultaneously. Then one
cadaverous looking woman
said *ah orgasms* and everyone
got all quiet and stood around
staring at their shoes. Such lovely
shoes. *Thank God for feet* said
the now naked minister, obviously
uncomfortable with the undeniable
fact of the all too human body.
The crazy girl with the fuck-
yourself eyes began to laugh
ecstatically. No one had ever
heard such divine laughter.
It seemed to well up out
of the ground as well as
fall out of the sky like
some terrible snow
or a blue rain, if there
had been a sky or ground
left to fall from or rise out of.

The weird laughter kept coming,
growing wilder and more intense
until it coalesced around them
in a dense cloud of shadow
swallowing every last thing
famously like a black hole
if a black hole could be said
to be famous. Then it ended
abruptly in a thunderous
round of silence.

The heart is a river

Everything empties into the ocean eventually.
Outside forces formed the ultimate boundaries,
not me. It was the surge that caused the flood
and the drought that brought the dry season.
The eddies and pools that you see here are
merely the progeny of a wanton motion.

What lasts is not rock, nor sky, nor water;
neither reflection nor pockmarked innuendo.
What lives on is only a dull sense of passing
and the ancient emptiness which is home
to both the systole and diastole of flowing

We wanted a way out

The dark was universal with only a little
moonlight leaking through the branches.
We were moving slowly, feeling our way
along what we imagined must be the path,
heading toward what we could only believe
would be a well lit, well marked road. The
night seems an eternity when you're this lost.
We had long since passed the graveyard
where the markers bore names like Nelson,
Permella, Eileen, Charles, and Dean. We
left that all behind now. We are sorry we
never meant to frighten you. We were
only looking for that thing we had all
been promised, but had so far eluded
us. That bright place where we could
finally forget and bathe in the pure light
of morning, but the woods are so thick
in these parts, and the wind is cold as
bone, and we can't see very well being
less than smoke. All we know is the snake
and the owl are gods in this realm of darkness,
flesh hunters both. Next time you come, please
bring a map or compass, a fire or flashlight,
or at least some small thing like a song
or a memory that will remind us
of what it means to be home.

In memory of my memory

The evening twits its wren-song
requiem to the backyard sunset
just as I remember my mother
perched on the perfect patio
of my memory, whistling
answers to the fragile
uncertainties gathering
beneath the darkening eaves.
Only a frozen moment outside
the thwack and holy, birdlike
flight of the well-struck
wiffleball, or the unstrung
voices of careless children
spilling about like over sloshed
lemonade, above the tinkle of ice
which is also embedded in this place
as if it were set like awkward feet
sunk in concrete. And here's father
home early from work, for once,
turning languidly through the sacred
sports section for a long since forgotten
score, the dry leaf crackle and the sudden
snap and flap like that of a wing being
surely beaten. There are odors here too
coming slowly like the neighbors'
ubiquitous barbeque, the tang
and thick sweetness mingling
with the ever present freshness
of resin from the storm-fallen
pine, mixed with the old oiled
tartness and insistent gas-burn
of the uncle-wielded chainsaw.
And other scents as well like maple
bacon beginning to wrinkle in the pan
or the bitterness of Sunday coffee
left on too long, or popcorn
and chicken paprika. Always
there's a slow enfolding warmth
like bed sheets newly drawn from
the rumbling of the Westinghouse
dryer, and steam ghosts rising

off of the long ago oared vacation
waters of childhood with its endless
vee trailing behind like a falling
veil until it, like everything
known, is given silently
back into mystery.

Under the influence

I was reading in the near dark
A Journal of the Year of the Ox

and thinking of you reading
perhaps these same words

thinking of the winter sky
bending from here to there

thinking of Wright's words-
how they shield and how thin

I feel thinking of January's
culling cold and dull snow

thinking of dissolving

until the light softens
and my eyes fail

Eternity

The words are on the page.
The page is in the book.
The book is on the shelf.
The shelf is in a library,
maybe it's Logansport,
in a section that smells
like history but is really
marked Poetry and, perhaps,
Philosophy. There it waits
until a young girl- classically-
-though not necessarily -
reaches to caress the spine,
could be on purpose, maybe
she likes something about
the title, or maybe it's all
a cosmic accident,
maybe she was reaching
for Bill Berkson, or some
one else and only pulls this
one out by mistake: but she
does anyway and she sits at
a table and opens the book
and begins to read, and, for less
than a second or so her breathing
changes, maybe her heart beats
differently, slows or speeds
at a turn of phrase or a leap
beyond faith, and she crosses
or uncrosses her long, graceful
legs, or they could be awkward
and ungainly but anyway there is
a moment like touching that manages
to happen, then she closes the book,
and takes it back to the shelf
and slips it back into place
beside Berkson or Bang or
Baraka, where again it waits.
The words are on the page,
all that is left of me.

Thanks and credits

I wish to thank the following: my wife and family for their love and support, my parents for having the good sense to have me, Dorothy Mienko for her constant friendship and encouragement, Ray Sweatman for his help and technical guidance, Golden, Alex, Blackford, Wendy and all my friends at *Cuttings*. Also, my friends and fellow poets at Salty. Finally, I wish to thank you, My Reader, even if you only exist in my mind.

Some of these poems first appeared in *Salamander, Belatrix Blue, Autumn Sky Poetry, Poetry Superhighway, and From East to West: Bicoastal Verse.*

The title for the book is from a quote by Oscar Wilde-

Seriousness is the only refuge of the shallow.

Front cover photo is *Espresso Bar, morning shadows* by brion berkshire.
Back cover photo is *brion, walking from water by* vali beyond.

www.ingramcontent.com/pod-product-compliance
Ingram Content Group UK Ltd.
Pitfield, Milton Keynes, MK11 3LW, UK
UKHW040558210726
13854UKWH00008B/1493